CAREERS *in Your Community*™

WORKING
as an
ELECTRICIAN
in YOUR COMMUNITY

Bobi Martin

rosen
PUBLISHING®

New York

Published in 2016 by The Rosen Publishing Group, Inc.
29 East 21st Street, New York, NY 10010

Copyright © 2016 by The Rosen Publishing Group, Inc.

First Edition

Library of Congress Cataloging-in-Publication Data

Martin, Bobi, author.
Working as an electrician in your community/Bobi Martin.—First edition.
    pages cm.—(Careers in your community)
Includes bibliographical references and index.
ISBN 978-1-4994-6111-4 (library bound)
1. Electricians—Juvenile literature. 2. Electrical engineering—Vocational guidance—Juvenile literature. [1. Occupations.] I. Title.
TK159.M37 2016
621.319'24'023
                                                              2014044185

Manufactured in the United States of America

Contents

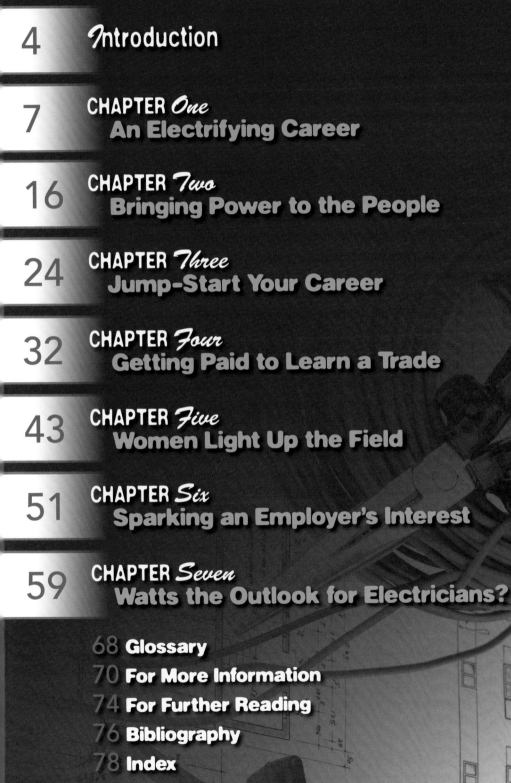

Introduction

After Hurricane Sandy flooded homes in in low-lying neighborhoods in and around New York City in 2012, thousands of people were left without power. Electricians scrambled to help, working twelve-hour days as they inspected homes for damage to panel boxes, restoring power where they could and making repairs where needed.

In February 2014, ice storms left tens of thousands of customers without power in Maryland, Pennsylvania, Georgia, and South Carolina. Electricians worked for days in frigid temperatures and dangerous conditions to restore heat and light. And when a 6.0 earthquake struck Napa, California, in August 2014, electricians were on the job almost as soon as the shaking stopped. They were able to restore power to some seventy thousand people within twenty-four hours.

Every year, communities across the country lose power following natural disasters like hurricanes, ice storms, earthquakes, tornados, and floods. Electricians work long hours in all kinds of weather to restore electricity again so people can see after dark, cook, keep food safely refrigerated, and have heat or air conditioning as they start rebuilding their homes and towns. At times like these, electricians are heroes in their communities.

But even in good times, we couldn't get by without electricians! Contractors need electricians to install

electrical components, wiring, circuit breakers, and switches when they build new homes, businesses, or factories. After the buildings are completed, electricians test circuits, electrical equipment, and power systems to make sure they are working safely.

Homeowners hire electricians to repair or replace faulty wiring, outdated circuit breakers, or damaged fuse boxes. When people install a security system, build additions to their homes,

After Hurricane Sandy, electricians in New York and neighboring areas worked long hours to test, repair, and replace electrical connections so families could have power again.

or add a swimming pool, they need electricians to install the new wiring and other electrical devices needed to power these things.

Maintenance electricians are always in demand at schools, hospitals, shopping centers, and factories. They inspect and test electrical equipment to make sure it is operating safely. If something is faulty, electricians replace the damaged parts to get things up and running again. And communities need electricians to work on such high tech equipment as computer, telecommunication, and robotics systems. The airline industry depends on aircraft electricians, and cities need electricians to keep their rapid transit systems functioning. In short, every area of our lives is touched by jobs electricians perform.

With electricians needed in so many areas, it's easy to see why the U.S. Department of Labor predicts that jobs for qualified electricians will grow faster than the average for all other occupations over the next decade!

Electricians enjoy interesting and challenging work that changes from day to day. If you like making things work, enjoy doing different tasks every day, and are pretty good at math, science, and problem solving, becoming an electrician could be the right choice for you. This career field is open to men and women and offers paid, on-the-job training. Whether you want to work inside or outdoors, want to be your own boss or prefer working for a company, a career as an electrician offers many exciting opportunities.

CHAPTER One

An Electrifying Career

Newspaper want ads and online job boards across the country list openings for many different kinds of electrician positions. Some job boards ask for residential electricians. Others have open industrial positions. Some ads request construction electricians. Don't they all do the same thing? Not exactly.

All electricians help install electricity in some way, but their job tasks—and job locations—can differ greatly. According to the Electrical Training Alliance, the largest national apprenticeship training program, there are four primary specialty areas for electricians. They are: residential wireman, inside wireman, installer technician, and outside lineman.

Because different communities have different needs, there are a wide variety of job opportunities within each of these main areas. Here is an overview of the primary specialty areas and a brief description of the job duties in each one.

Residential Wireman

A residential wireman works in new home construction and with existing homes. He or she may work on single family homes or on multifamily dwellings such as duplexes, condominiums, or apartment buildings.

New Construction

Contractors in every community depend on residential wiremen when they are building new dwellings. Once the framework of a home is in place, a residential wireman studies the blueprint (a technical diagram) that shows where outlets, circuits, and other components will be located. Sometimes the wireman helps plan the best placement of outlets, heating and air conditioning systems, and light fixtures.

Because she or he is responsible for making sure that electrical power is safely distributed from the home to the outside power source, the wireman may also plan where the grounding conductors and connections must go, and where the circuit breaker box should be installed. All of this requires knowledge of local building codes as well as safety regulations such as those outlined in the National Electric Code.

Residential wiremen run conduit and thread wiring. They install outlets, switches, relays, and circuit breaker panel boxes. They wire the electrical systems that power appliances and other electronic equipment. They are also responsible for testing the function and continuity of the home's circuits and components to ensure they function properly and safely.

Installing outlets and wall sockets involves more than just wiring. Electricians test each unit to ensure that it is receiving current and is properly grounded.

Existing Dwellings

Individual homeowners in every community depend on residential wiremen, too. The wiring in older homes may become worn or outdated. An electrician will run tests using special equipment such as ohmmeters, voltmeters, or oscilloscopes to see if the wiring can be repaired or needs to be replaced.

Even in fairly new homes, adding new appliances or electronic systems may require more power than the existing wire can safely carry. Homeowners who remodel their home or build an addition rely on residential wiremen to install the new wiring, outlets, ceiling fans, and lighting fixtures.

Homeowners also hire electricians to install power for security systems, computer networking, and other systems. Residential wiremen are also called out when a home loses power, whether that is due to a problem with a circuit breaker or due to a storm or other natural disaster.

CLIMBING THE CAREER LADDER

Job titles in advertisements vary depending on the type of electrical work to be done, where that work will be performed, and the level of experience wanted. The descriptions below are general titles that indicate increasing knowledge and job experience.

Electrician's helper: This is someone who is just entering the trade and is not enrolled in an apprenticeship program. Helpers start off performing duties that require little skill. They work under the close supervision of a qualified electrician.

Apprentice electrician: An apprentice works on electrical systems under the supervision of a journey-man electrician. Apprentices must complete 144 hours of classroom training and 2,000 hours of paid, on-the-job training each year. They receive periodic increases in pay as their skills and responsibilities increase. Apprenticeship programs last four to five years, depending on the type of program.

Journeyman electrician: A journeyman has com-pleted an apprenticeship program. He or she works without direct supervision and may supervise appren-tice electricians or helpers. Many states require a journeyman to pass a test and become licensed.

Lead: A lead is a journeyman who supervises one or more small crews of other journeymen, apprentices, and helpers. Leads work from prepared plans and report to a supervisor.

Area supervisor: This is an experienced journeyman who schedules workers and supervises one or more leads or crews. Area supervisors plan the order of the work to be done and are responsible for having the right materials, tools, and equipment at the job site.

Project supervisor: This is an experienced journey-man who is responsible for all of the employees on a project. Project supervisors oversee the work on the project and ensure schedules are met.

Master electrician: Many states require a master electrician to have at least seven years of journeyman experience. Some states require an electrical contractor to be a certified master electrician.

Commercial and Industrial Electricians

Commercial businesses like shopping centers and apartment complexes, and industries such as manufacturing plants and factories, are major employers in many communities. To keep everything— and everyone—working, they depend on electricians to install, test, maintain, and repair equipment and machinery. According to the Bureau of Labor Statistics, factories provide the most stable employment for electricians. This may be due to the need for most

To prevent costly shutdowns, maintenance electricians in factories and manufacturing plants inspect and test breaker boxes and other equipment to ensure they are operating correctly.

factories to operate twenty-four hours a day, seven days a week. Commercial and industrial electricians may be inside wiremen or outside linemen, which are sometimes called outside wiremen.

Inside Wireman

Inside wiremen work with businesses or industries. They often install power for large machinery that requires heavy-duty electronic components. They pull cables as well as groups of wires through large conduits and may also install light fixtures, outlets, alarm systems, and control panels. They may work with electrical motors or electronic equipment.

Many inside wiremen are maintenance electricians who perform preventative maintenance procedures such as testing equipment to ensure it is continuing to operate safely. They also repair transformers, motors, generators, and industrial robotic equipment. Electricians who work for a large company often work as part of a crew.

Inside wiremen enjoy varied tasks. One day they might be working on heating equipment, and the next day they might be installing a robotic system or repairing wiring.

Installer Technician

Installer technicians generally work alongside inside wiremen. They are responsible for installing the network of low voltage cables that are used for video, voice, and data signaling systems such as those used for climate control, telephone, security, and other communications equipment, including voice-activated systems. They may work in new construction or in an existing facility.

Typical duties on a job for a business include installing voice and data outlets at individual workstations, routing voice and data cables from telephone rooms to individual workstations, and installing cross connects or punch down blocks in telephone rooms. Installer technicians may also work with fiber optics.

Installer technicians also diagnose problems with equipment and may be responsible for

Linemen work with high voltage wires and need to be able to climb up power poles that can be 40 to 60 feet (12 to 18 meters) tall.

repairing and maintaining audio visual or video data equipment. They may also be called voice/data/video (VDV) electricians or integrated building systems (IBS) electricians.

Outside Lineman

Outside linemen work in all types of weather to install and maintain the transmission lines that bring electricity from power plants to homes, businesses, and industries. They are responsible for installing and maintaining transformers, towers, insulators, and substations. They also work on street lights and traffic signals.

Outside linemen are vital to maintaining existing power systems, as well as installing additional systems and substations as the needs of a community grow. When power is knocked out within a neighborhood or a city due to storms or other causes, outside linemen brave the elements to get things working again.

Whether they work inside or outside, work for construction or in maintenance, electricians at all levels are valued and needed in every community.

CHAPTER Two

Bringing Power to the People

During new construction, electricians install panel boxes, outlets, and other electrical systems. They also run the wires that provide electrical power to the building.

Communities can't function without electrical power. And power can't be brought to residents and businesses without electricians. We may be "wireless" in many ways, but we need electricians to keep us connected! This is especially true as communities grow and new technologies continue to be developed.

In fact, despite the development of solar energy, wind power, and other alternative energy sources, our demands for electricity continue to increase. According to an article from the National

Academy of Sciences, "Experts predict a 35% increase in demand for electricity by 2030." And that means an increased need for electricians across the country.

TESLA AND EDISON'S WAR OF THE CURRENTS

Nikola Tesla and Thomas Edison brought amazing developments to the world through their inventions. Both of these brilliant inventors also contributed to bringing the use of electricity to communities. Although many people credit Edison as the better inventor, that issue is still hotly debated.

Tesla worked for Edison for a time, but the two men disliked each other and disagreed about many things. Their most famous feud is known as the War of Currents. Edison felt that his system of direct current (DC) was safer and vastly superior to Tesla's alternating current (AC) system. This was primarily due to the fact that direct current maintained a low voltage from the power station to people's homes. But a major drawback of DC was that homes and businesses had to be within one mile of a power station.

Tesla's AC system allowed electrical current to change direction, making it more practical for cities, which needed to move large amounts of current over larger distances. But Tesla had no power plant or power stations. American inventor and businessman George Westinghouse agreed with Tesla's ideas. He built an AC

(continued on the next page)

Tesla had a number of labs, including this one, where he and George Westinghouse developed a way to deliver AC energy over long distances.

(continued from the previous page)

power plant at Niagara Falls that powered New York City, and AC won out in popularity. The power grid we use today is similar to that first one.

But we use Edison's DC system, too. Since common household appliances can't handle huge amounts of AC energy, most of our electrical devices have an internal component that converts AC into safer, lower voltage DC.

Physical and Mental Demands

So what does it take to be an electrician? While you don't need to be a body builder, you do need to be in good physical condition, and you should also have good physical and mental stamina. No matter what their area of specialty, most electricians spend long periods of time on their feet. They may have to lift or hold heavy tools for a length of time while working. They may also have to carry heavy equipment or tools from one part of the job to another, including moving these items up or down a ladder or stairs. Mental stamina is important because electricians often need to focus intently on a particular task despite other distractions. Some tasks may require their full attention for a long period of time.

Flexibility and Balance

Flexibility and a good sense of balance are important, too. Electricians sometimes have to bend, twist, or hold an awkward position while working. They may have to reach up or out with their arms or legs to reach the area they are working on. Some jobs require stooping, squatting, or kneeling for an extended time, or working in a tight or confined area. Electricians sometimes have to crawl through low or narrow spaces to install, replace, or repair conduit or wiring.

Good balance is important since electricians may need to work while standing on scaffolding, ladders, or platforms. They may work on high areas such as rooftops or on high floors of buildings under construction. Outside linemen regularly work at great heights and may need to climb tall poles or towers to reach the area to be worked on.

Dexterity and Coordination

Electricians need nimble fingers as some jobs require threading thin wires through small conduit, working with small connectors, or handling very tiny screws. Those working with electronic components may have to splice or cap very delicate wire ends. Attaching or assembling small parts, wires, screws, and connectors requires good finger and hand dexterity.

It is also important for electricians to be able to maintain steadiness in their hands and arms while working with wires, tools, and equipment. This includes being able to move both hands and arms together in a coordinated way while positioning or manipulating wires, tools, or equipment. And because

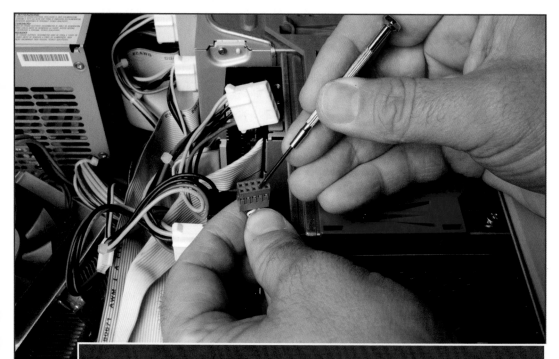

Electricians need a steady hand and keen eyesight when they are working on electronic components that have tiny screws and connectors.

of the risk of shock or burns, it is also important for an electrician to be able to move their fingers, hands, arms, legs, or body quickly.

Some job sites may have several people working in the same area or working together on the same task. Electricians must be able to adjust their actions to coordinate with the movement of others around them.

Vision

Because electricians work with color-coded wires, good color vision is essential. Electricians not only work with different colors of wire but also must sometimes distinguish between shades of similar colors such as pale grey and white. Or they may need to choose between different brightness, such as pale yellow and deeper yellow. Attaching the wrong wires can result in a burn or a nasty shock to themselves or others, as well as damage to equipment or wiring.

Some work areas are small or narrow, so it is also helpful to have good near vision, the ability to see things within a few inches to a few feet. Reading work-related documents such as repair or installation manuals, blueprints, and other instructions in poor light requires good vision as well.

Dangers and Safety Concerns

Every occupation carries some risk of injury. Common injuries for electricians include shocks, burns, falls, and other minor injuries. Although few of these injuries are fatal, the U.S. Department of Labor reports that electricians have a higher rate of injuries and illnesses than the national average for work-related injuries. Using protective gear such as gloves, hearing protection, hard hats, and safety glasses reduces the risk of harm.

Work conditions for electricians can be challenging. An electrician may sometimes work in a ditch or in damp or wet conditions. Maintenance electricians deal with grease and oil, while other jobs are performed in dusty, dirty, or hot areas. Outside linemen are exposed to various weather conditions, from extreme cold during an ice storm to sweltering heat during the summer months.

When a Nebraska snowstorm brought sub-zero temperatures, electricians used a blowtorch to thaw an electrical connector.

Some job sites, such as factories and assembly plants, may be constantly noisy. Construction electricians are exposed to noises from high-powered saws and nail guns. Commercial and industrial electricians work around noisy equipment and machines.

Important Qualities

Electricians need a number of skills and qualities to perform their jobs successfully. Two of these are troubleshooting and critical-thinking skills.

For example, frustrated homeowners might call an electrician because their homes lost power, and they want their lights and power back on quickly. But the cause of the problem may be due to more than one thing. The electrician must be able to analyze the situation to find the most logical cause of the problem and then determine which tests to run in order to confirm the diagnosis and make the proper repairs.

Similarly, when a machine or piece of equipment in a factory breaks down and stops production, maintenance electricians are under pressure to determine the cause quickly and get things up and running as soon as possible. An electrician with good troubleshooting and critical-thinking skills can find and resolve the problem in a timely manner. This can save a company from losing thousands of dollars due to lost production time.

CHAPTER Three

Jump-Start Your Career

Working with electricity can be dangerous. This is one reason why apprenticeship positions for this career field last four to five years, as opposed to much shorter training for many other careers. But many electricians can't picture themselves doing anything else. Electricians are wanted in every community, and there are dozens of job specialties to choose from.

Jennifer Aquila, an aviation electrician in Indiana who works on the electrical systems of aircraft for AAR, a company that offers services and products for aircraft, says, "It's a challenging field, but it's also fun and exciting. As long as you are willing to learn and aren't afraid to get your hands dirty, the opportunities are endless."

General Classes

Future electricians can jump-start their career while they are in middle school or high school. One way to do this is by taking courses they will need later. In addition to a high school diploma or a general educational development (GED) diploma, a basic requirement for nearly all apprenticeship programs is a year of algebra.

Technicians should know how to study blueprints, which show how the wiring and switches in the fuse box are connected and what they control.

Other math classes are also important. Electricians use basic math skills including percentages, fractions, and determining the area of a multisided figure, as well as consumer math skills. Because electricians frequently work with blueprints and schematics, mechanical drawing and drafting courses will help, too.

Most high schools or local community colleges offer industrial arts and shop classes. These, in addition to basic high school chemistry and physics classes, will also give future electricians an edge. And with an eye toward safety, taking a first aid course that includes cardiopulmonary resuscitation (CPR) could impress a future employer. Most communities offer CPR as well as basic and advanced first aid classes through their local Red Cross.

Vo-Tech and CTE

Another way to jump-start a career as an electrician is enrolling in a vocational technical school, often called

STAYING SAFE AT WORK

An article by the National Institute for Occupational Safety and Health (NIOSH) reported that about 18.1 million workers in 2013 were younger than twenty-four years old. According to the article, "The rate for emergency department–treated occupational injuries of young workers was approximately two times higher than among workers 25 years and older."

To help reduce injuries in the electrical and construction trades, NIOSH has published a student manual titled *Electrical Safety: Safety and Health for Electrical Trades*. The book was developed with the help of vocational instructors, and it is heavily illustrated with photographs and real-life work examples. It is available for free and may be downloaded from the NIOSH website.

vo-tech, or in a career and technical education (CTE) school. Vo-tech and CTE schools are available across the country. In some areas, a CTE or vo-tech program is on the campus of a traditional high school. In others, it has its own campus.

These schools offer teens the ability to earn their high school diploma while studying specific courses related to their future careers. It is also a great way to explore a career field to see if it is a good fit. Career-related classes for future electricians typically include electrical theory, technical math, blueprint reading, circuitry, courses in the fundamentals of electrical wiring, and work safety.

Most vocational and CTE schools also include lab classes that give students the opportunity to receive valuable hands-on training in work-related skills. For

Electrical vo-tech programs give students an opportunity to work with electrical circuitry and to handle some tools of the trade in a safe environment.

electrician students, that might include building circuits, splicing wires, and soldering. Lab classes also give students experience in using tools they'll work with in the future. Another advantage of CTE and vo-tech schools is that their core curriculum classes are integrated to connect with the career a student is pursuing. This helps make classes in math, reading, science, and other subjects more relevant to students.

Many CTE and vocational schools have relationships with local electrical contractors or other electrical businesses in their community that may offer on-the-job training opportunities for senior students. *The Occupational Outlook Handbook*, published by the Bureau of Labor Statistics, states, "Employers often hire students who complete these programs and usually start them at a more advanced level than those without this training."

College or Apprenticeship?

A college degree is not necessary to become an electrician. Some people take a short trade school or college program first, but the majority of electricians begin their career through an apprenticeship program. However, a number of apprenticeship programs award college credits toward an associate's or bachelor's degree. And those who plan to become self-employed or who want to start a contracting business often take additional business classes through a local or online college.

Most states require electricians to be licensed, which can involve passing an exam on their knowledge of state or local building codes and the National Electric Code. So, even after completing an apprenticeship program, many electricians continue taking

Most tech schools offer lab classes so students can practice what they have learned by working on sample equipment, such as these panel boxes.

classes to stay current on changes to these codes. Electricians may also take classes to learn about new systems or special equipment their employers want to use, or to keep up with changes in the needs of their customers. The National Joint Apprenticeship and Training Committee (NJATC) says that new demands created by technologies such as fiber-optic communications, computer networking, fire and security alarm systems, and others means that residential wiremen will need to take classes to stay current in their field.

Still others take classes with an eye toward becoming a contractor. A January 2014 article published by the U.S. Department of Labor says that some states require an electrical contractor to be a certified master electrician. Additionally, most states require master electricians to have either a bachelor's degree in

THE JOB CORPS

Another avenue to starting a career as an electrician is the Job Corps. For low-income young people who are between sixteen and twenty-four years old, the Job Corps can be life changing. Job Corps offers young men and women the opportunity to earn their high school diploma or GED and to be trained in one of more than a hundred career areas, including the electrical field. There is no cost to students who are accepted into the program, which is administered by the U.S. Department of Labor.

Students may live at home or in housing provided by Job Corps. Along with job skills, young people are taught the life skills they need in order to be successful in stable, long-term, and well-paying jobs. This includes courses in independent living, interviewing, and social skills. Medical and dental care is provided, as is a living and clothing allowance. Some Job Corps centers offer child care programs for single parents.

Job Corps has 125 campuses across the United States and in Puerto Rico. The program has helped more than 2.7 million young people.

electrical engineering, or a related field, or to have at least seven years of experience.

Another way to explore an electrical career is through a local Young Worker group, where teens can meet young men and women electricians. This can provide the opportunity to learn firsthand about different types of electrical careers and to get helpful advice.

Sponsored by various state and local union councils, Young Worker groups can be found across the United States and Canada. Some, such as the Young Workers of California, the Colorado Young Worker Project, and Minnesota Young Workers, have their own Facebook pages.

Tarn Goelling, the chairperson of the Washington, D.C., chapter of Young Trade Unionists (YTU), says, "Many young worker groups around the United States and Canada have active International Brotherhood of Electrical Workers (IBEW) members, as well as other trades and union members. Teens can make contacts with members who are electricians and learn about local apprenticeship programs through those individuals."

From enrolling in a local CTE or vo-tech school to reaching out to a nearby Young Worker group, there are many local opportunities for teens to start working toward a career as an electrician.

CHAPTER Four

Getting Paid to Learn a Trade

Who would pass up the opportunity to get paid while learning their trade? Getting a head start on a career is exciting, and there are several ways to earn a paycheck while working toward your career goal. Best of all, most of these opportunities are available in every community.

Many high school students work part-time during the school year or at a full-time position over summer break. Several kinds of part-time jobs can help teens learn about the types of tools, equipment, or electrical parts electricians work with. Jobs at local retail businesses that sell electrical parts and tools, building supply stores, and parts supply stores offer work

Many part-time jobs, such as a position in a store where hand tools are sold, can help high school students prepare for a career as an electrician.

experience and a chance to become familiar with the tools of an electrician's trade.

A local contractor or electrical business may have part-time positions available as well. Christopher Lee is a licensed contractor and the owner of Electrical-Etc., which provides residential, commercial, and industrial electrical services in Arizona and California. Lee says, "Part-time positions for teens could include shop help, or stocking vehicles and trailers to get to know the materials."

Electrician's Helper

Lee's company, and many others, may also hire teens for a full-time position during the summer as an electrician's helper. According to Lee, "The minimum age for the helper's position is 16 years old, and they would have to have parental consent and a driver's license."

Electrician's helper positions are available in every state, according to information provided by the Bureau of Labor Statistics. Electrician's helpers work under the supervision of an apprentice or journeyman electrician and generally perform duties that do not require much knowledge of electricity, such as holding or retrieving tools, cleaning equipment or the work area, and transporting tools, materials, and equipment to the work site.

The position usually also provides the chance to perform tasks that introduce the helper to working with tools and testing equipment. Some of those tasks may include:

- *Using hand tools and other instruments to measure, cut, and bend wire and conduit*
- *Using hand and power tools to drill holes and thread wiring through the openings*
- *Using wire-stripping pliers to strip insulation from the wire ends*
- *Using a soldering gun to attach wires to terminals*
- *Using a test meter to locate short circuits in wiring*
- *Using saws, drill presses, taps, and power drills to construct panels and controllers*

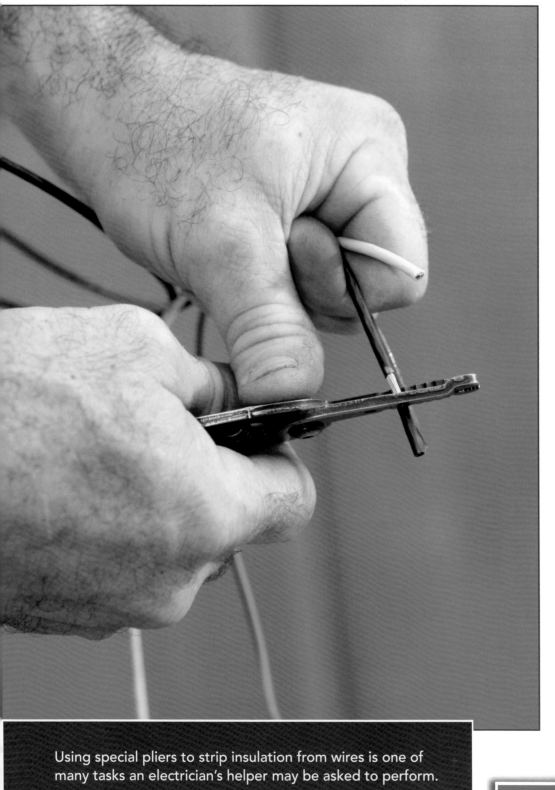

Using special pliers to strip insulation from wires is one of many tasks an electrician's helper may be asked to perform.

Newspapers sometimes list advertisements for a shop helper or for an electrician's helper, and local employment offices also post available job openings. Contacting a local business or union could provide a job lead as well.

Apprenticeship Programs

The vast majority of electrical workers in the United States and Canada learn their trade through a four- to five-year apprenticeship program. Such training programs can be found in many communities, and information about them can also be easily located on the Internet. Trade associations such as the Independent Electrical Contractors (IEC), labor unions such as the IBEW and NJATC, and other organizations like the Canadian Electrical Contractors Association (CECA) offer apprenticeship programs in various locations. Generally, the basic requirements for an apprentice program are:

- *Minimum age of eighteen*
- *High school or GED diploma*
- *One year of algebra*

Some programs also require passing an aptitude test and clearing a drug screening test.

Apprenticeship programs include paid, on-the-job training, combined with classroom instruction. For each year of the program, an apprentice must clock at least 2,000 hours on the job and must receive 144 hours of classroom instruction.

Apprentices work under the direct supervision of experienced electricians or contractors. Coursework

Journeyman electricians guide apprentices as they learn how to perform various tasks. Apprentices may work with a number of journeymen during their program.

is designed to match what the apprentice will be doing, or needs to know, on the job at different phases of the program. Topics become more complex as the apprentice advances.

Similarly, job duties increase in difficulty as the apprentice works through the program. While apprentices are not paid a great deal at the start of their apprenticeship, they receive regular salary increases as they successfully complete each phase of the program.

TOOLS TO INVEST IN

Most employers generally provide large tools like conduit benders, as well as equipment such as test meters and power tools, but electricians must have their own hand tools. This can be a major investment to an apprentice just starting out. In *The Complete Idiot's Guide to Electronics 101*, authors Sean Westcott and Jean Riescher Westcott stress the importance of investing in good tools. "Good hand tools will last a lifetime," they write. "Spend a little extra to get the best quality instruments you can afford."

On his website, Electrician Information Resource, Dusten Huebner, a Canadian industrial electrician, agrees that having the right tools is important. But he cautions new helpers and apprentices to be frugal when they're starting out. "Many first time rookie electricians feel that they need to buy top of the line tools, but as long as your tools are sturdy, you don't have to spend a fortune," he writes.

Some basic tools many electricians use include the following:

- **Banana knife** *For stripping cable and insulation.*
- **Cable cutters** *To cut large conductors and some smaller cables.*
- **Channel locks** *Pliers that grip different objects. Electricians will usually need several different sizes.*

- **Electrician scissors** *For cutting thick gauged wire.*
- **Electrician's screwdrivers** *Flat-heads and Phillips screwdrivers that protect against shocks while working on electrical systems. Usually needed in several sizes.*
- **Metric hex keys** *For tightening electrical termination lugs.*
- **Multimeter** *For testing AC/DC volts, amps, and resistance.*
- **Pliers** *Electricians use needle nose, long nose, crimping, and lineman's pliers. Each does a different job, usually involving the handling of wires.*
- **Side cutters** *For cutting smaller wires and tie wraps.*
- **Wire cutters** *For cutting wires. High-quality blades are worth the extra cost. A "stand-off shear" won't deform the wire. Usually needed*

Electricians use multimeters to find trouble spots in a circuit or to test voltage, current, and resistance of components such as capacitors, diodes, and transistors.

(continued on the next page)

(continued from the previous page)

in several sizes.
- **Wire strippers** *To cut insulation from coated wire without cutting the wire itself. Good quality strippers have gauge holes for different gauges of wire.*

Some general tools electricians use are a socket set, wrench set, tape measure, hack saw, magnetized torpedo level, and hammer. Tool belts help electricians keep track of their tools, and a pouch with several pockets is useful for holding screws and other small parts.

After successfully completing the program, an apprentice becomes a journeyman. Most states require a journeyman to be licensed, which can involve providing proof of completion of an approved apprenticeship and passing a test.

Military Training

Another way to earn a salary while learning the electrician trade is through the military. Jennifer Aquila began her career this way. "After a full day of testing and physicals, I sat down with a Navy recruiter who went over all the jobs my test results had qualified me for. I chose Aviation Electricians Mate (AE) because I've always loved airplanes and figuring out how they worked interested me."

Just like communities everywhere, all branches of the U.S. military, including the Coast Guard and National Guard, and the Canadian Armed Forces

As an electrician in the National Guard, Staff Sgt. Fran Dixon has performed a number of duties, including replacing runway lights on a flight line.

need electricians. Similar to an apprenticeship, military men and women who are selected to become electricians will receive classroom instruction and on-the-job training.

Aquila says, "I had to pass a two month basic electricians course, where I learned the theory and mathematics behind electricity, and then a three month course in aviation electronics." This was followed by hands-on training working in the aviation electricians shop. The skills and training Aquila received during her military career enabled her to quickly find a position after her service ended. "I was surprised by how easy it was to find a job," she says. "My military experience was a big selling point."

From part-time jobs during the school year to summers working as an electrician's helper, teens have multiple ways to earn while they learn. After graduation, a stint in the military or enrollment in an apprenticeship program is a good way to get paid, on-the-job training for a career as an electrician.

CHAPTER Five

Women Light Up the Field

Women have been working as electricians since the late 1970s. Back then, a career in the trades was so nontraditional for women that almost every one of them experienced harassment that aimed to push them out of the field. Although the electrical trade is still considered a nontraditional career for women today, that perception is finally beginning to change. There are now many women electricians throughout

Construction electricians consult blueprints to see where to install circuit boxes. They also drill holes through studs and thread conduit and electric wiring.

the United States and Canada—and a number of them own their own business.

Being Your Own Boss

After working for many years in another career, Joann Greeley decided to join her father and uncle in the electrical trade in Newfoundland, Canada. But first she took the time to prepare for the career switch. "I took a nine month trade course before entering my apprenticeship," she says. While working as an apprentice, and later as a journeyman electrician, she performed all types of electrical work, including commercial and industrial, before she decided to become self-employed as a residential wireman.

Her business, Joann Greeley Electric, provides various installation and repair services for homeowners. Greeley loves her career. "I get to use my brain all the time. I make great money, and I work for myself," she says.

She finds that a woman-owned business has a definite advantage because many women feel more comfortable having a female electrician come into their home. "About 90% of my clients are women," Greeley says. "Women make most of the choices when it comes to upgrades in a home. They would rather hire a woman when they can because we listen to them, and we work more neatly."

Contributing to the Community

Jasmine Bush is a twenty-four-year-old journeyman inside wireman in Connecticut. Like most electricians, she loves being able to work with her hands and takes great pride in the work she does as an electrician in her community. "I enjoy driving past a job and telling my friends and family, 'I helped build that,'" she says.

Bush says going to a vo-tech high school helped her decide to become an electrician. "Vo-tech schools allow you to explore all of the trades that they offer. I was actually interested in fashion first, but after exploring electrical I just knew that it was what I wanted to do," she says. After finishing her apprenticeship, Bush enrolled in Southern New Hampshire University's online program to work toward a bachelor's degree in technical management.

At many vo-tech schools, students can explore different careers. This student is practicing how to wire a utility control panel.

While some women electricians today still report being harassed on the job, Bush says, "I've never had any big problems; mostly everyone has treated me like a sister. As long as you keep your head held high and you do your job, you shouldn't have many problems."

Jennifer Aquila agrees. "Both during my career in the military and now in civilian aviation, I have never experienced any harassment. But I have found that being female usually puts an extra level of scrutiny on your abilities. I don't let that bother me; I just do my job and after a couple of days I'm treated like all the rest."

PROTECTING THE RIGHTS OF WORKING WOMEN

The Women's Bureau is one of the oldest agencies in the U.S. Department of Labor. It was established in 1920 to promote the rights and welfare of working women. Some of its goals include making women aware of their rights in the workplace and designing laws and policies that promote the interests and needs of working women.

A highlight of the agency's history is the inclusion of women's work under the terms of the 1938 Fair Labor Standards Act, which set the minimum wage a worker can be paid and the maximum hours employees can be made to work for that amount of pay. The Women's Bureau also helped pass the Equal Pay Act, which was signed into law by President John F. Kennedy in 1963. Before the EPA was passed, women were often paid less than men who were doing the same job under the same conditions.

Another major focus of the organization has been recruiting women to nontraditional jobs in such trades as construction and electrical, as well as other areas that pay higher wages than the types of lower-paying positions often offered to women.

Proving Grounds

"Male or female, once you prove yourself as an apprentice it is way easier," says Calli Doucette, a fourth-year electrical apprentice working for the International Brotherhood of Electrical Workers (IBEW), local 303, in Ontario, Canada. "As an apprentice you don't get the cleanest or easiest job because you need to prove that you want to be there."

Doucette's interest in a job working with her hands began while helping her father, a millwright and welder, build and fix things around their farm. "Dad always told me that there were women electricians on his job,"

Women who like working with their hands and solving problems may enjoy the electrical field. Some women electricians operate their own businesses.

she says. In high school she took a Specialist High Skills Major (SHSM) course in construction. During the course, she, along with twenty other students, helped build a house from start to finish for Habitat for Humanity. "This is where I really knew I wanted to be in the electrical trade," she says.

She also took a one-year Electrician Pre-Trade program through a local college prior to applying for an apprenticeship with IBEW. Doucette works mainly in commercial settings where she says she does everything from running pipe, pulling wire, and slab work to installing solar farms, security systems, and fire alarm systems.

Like Joann Greeley, journeyman Lisa Langevin spent many years in another profession before making a career switch. "I wanted a job with some thinking involved, which paid well, and had good benefits," she says. With a mortgage and other bills to pay, Langevin also needed a career that allowed her to earn a salary as she learned her new craft. After taking a ten-month pre-apprentice course at British Columbia Institute of Technology, she applied for an apprenticeship with IBEW, local 213, and was placed in a position at Mott Electric.

Langevin says she experienced some harassment as an apprentice but adds, "Some guys, the bullies, take advantage of all newbies whether they are men or women. The majority of guys, once they realize you can do the job, don't really care if you are a man or a woman."

As an electrician, Langevin does everything from installing lights and data jacks to installing public announcement systems and helping build new stores. She not only enjoys making things work but

Male or female, electricians must be good at problem solving and working with others. Journeyman electricians help apprentices learn how to analyze problems to come up with the best solution.

also feels a sense of satisfaction from doing a job that contributes to her community.

"A couple of years ago I helped fully renovate the YMCA in downtown Vancouver," she says. "I ran most of the 4" pipe in the building, and I love knowing that for years to come, that pipe will still be there doing its job."

According to Langevin, many opportunities are available to women electricians who want to advance in their career. "After you have been in the trade for some time, you can move into many different positions such as estimating, project management, or inspecting," she says.

Filling the Gap

With many older electricians retiring and the demand for electrical workers increasing, there is a growing shortfall of electricians in both the United States and Canada. Currently, in both countries, women make up less than 2 percent of employed electricians, according to an article by Catalyst, a nonprofit organization dedicated to expanding opportunities for women and business.

With more women than men in the work force, attracting young women to the electrician field could be the solution to a growing problem. Mia Rivas, a journeyman inside wireman in California, says, "This is an awesome career! I make good money and have great benefits." Jasmine Bush agrees. "If you are thinking about becoming an electrician, there's no time like the present."

CHAPTER Six

Sparking an Employer's Interest

It's an age-old problem. Employers want workers with experience, but workers can't get experience until someone hires them. So how does a teen with no job experience get an interview and then land the job?

Finding a Job

First, you have to find a job to apply for. One way to do that is through networking. Many CTE and vo-tech schools have working relationships with electrical contractors, unions, or other businesses in the community. A teacher or career counselor at these schools can help students contact those businesses to ask about job openings. Young Worker groups provide an opportunity to network with apprentice and journeyman electricians in the community, as well as with local union representatives who may know of job openings.

Career counselors help job applicants learn how to fill out an application in a way that makes a strong first impression.

A common networking trick many job seekers use is simply letting people know they are looking for work. They tell friends, neighbors, teachers, friends of the family—in short, just about everyone they know—that they are looking for a job. Many times one of these people will know of a company with a job opening.

Looking in the newspaper and checking with the local employment office are two other common ways of finding job openings. Some employment offices have staff on hand who can assist first-time job seekers with their job search as well as with filling out a job application. Many of these postings might also be online.

Temporary agencies in the community are another possibility. As the name suggests, these companies help place workers in temporary jobs. Some positions are very short term, lasting only a few days, while other positions may last a month or longer. An advantage of working with temporary agencies is that they work with companies that do not advertise job openings elsewhere. Working with a temporary agency also lets young workers try different positions, while gaining experience to put on a résumé. Sometimes a temporary position leads to a long-term job offer.

What Is a Résumé?

A résumé is a job seeker's best tool to tell potential employers about themselves. For most young adults, a résumé will be only one page long. It should list the job seeker's contact information, work or volunteer experience, job skills, and education.

First-time job seekers often have more to put on a résumé than they realize. A paper route, babysitting, or doing yard work or other odd jobs for neighbors count as work experience. Even if there was no payment involved, such jobs still demonstrate responsibility. Volunteer experience could include things such as helping at a food bank or the local SPCA, scouting, being on Student Council at school, or working on a Habitat for Humanity project.

Under education, a teen should list the grade he or she is in, as well as the name of his or her current school. Mention perfect attendance at school or at a volunteer position, as this shows potential employers that the job seeker is dependable. Job skills can include such things as being able to use a computer,

Robotics competitions like this one, sponsored by MIT, and others, like Lego League's First Robotics Competition, are fun ways to learn about aspects of electrical work.

being knowledgeable about common word processing and spreadsheet applications, knowing how to use hand tools, and so on.

List any hobbies that are related in some way to the job position. For example, repairing radios, building model electric trains, or building electronics kits involve some of the same skills that electricians use. Other related activities might include participating at a local Lego League robotics competition or working with a local ham radio group.

Résumés that are neatly typed with no spelling errors create a positive first impression. It is also best to use a clean, simple font. Avoid fancy fonts and large type as this looks unprofessional. Many public libraries have books on résumé writing that include examples of different types of résumés. Numerous websites, which can be found through a basic web search, offer free résumé templates along with tips for creating effective résumés.

Interviewing

Many people feel nervous when they go to an interview. Rehearsing with an adult ahead of time will help build confidence. Practice walking into the room, making direct eye contact with the interviewer, and smiling while giving the interviewer a firm handshake. This creates a very positive first impression. To avoid stammering or having awkward pauses filled with "uhms" and "ahs" during an interview, practice answering a variety of questions.

It is also smart to learn something about the company and the industry before the interview. According to human resources professional Lin Grensing-Pophal,

Practice interviews help young job seekers learn how to make good impressions with prospective employers, starting with the opening handshake.

an interviewer is likely to ask a few questions that are designed to see what the job seeker knows about the company or the industry. Most businesses have a website that gives a bit of their history, along with a statement explaining what the company's values are. Savvy job seekers take the time to learn as much as they can about the company so that they are well prepared for their interview.

At the end of an interview, most hiring managers ask the job seeker if they have any questions. Grensing-Pophal warns against asking about money or job perks before being offered the job. Smart questions to ask include: What are you looking for in your ideal

DRESSING FOR SUCCESS

More than one job seeker has lost the job because he or she was dressed inappropriately for the interview. Spiked hair, face piercings, and an outfit that looks better suited for attending a rock concert certainly creates an impression—but not the kind that gets a person hired.

In her book, *Interview Success—Get the Edge*, job consultant Julie Gray offers tips for creating a positive first impression. "The interviewer will assess how you look (and smell), behave, and communicate," she writes. Gray recommends simple hair styles and avoiding strong aftershave or perfume. She also suggests removing any piercings except for earrings, and keeping tattoos covered if possible.

Dress appropriately for where the interview will take place. There is no need to wear a suit to a construction site, but ripped jeans and a T-shirt are not suitable either. A pair of khakis or dark slacks and an ironed shirt or blouse is fine. Girls should avoid wearing short skirts, revealing tops, or fancy heels.

Lin Grensing-Pophal, a certified human resources professional, also stresses the importance of appearance in her book *The Everything Job Interview Book*: "Arriving for an interview too casually dressed tells the interviewer that you don't care enough about the job or the company to put your best self forward."

candidate? Are there opportunities to advance in this position? When do you think you will be making a hiring decision?

Don't forget to ask for the job. This may sound odd, but many interviewers say the majority of people they interview fail to indicate any meaningful interest in the position. This is easily and smoothly handled while getting up to leave. When reaching out to shake the hiring manager's hand, a simple, "Thank-you for meeting with me. I'd love to come to work for your company!" conveys interest in the position.

After the Interview

Sending a thank-you letter after an interview is another way to create a positive impression. Job seekers should follow up by immediately e-mailing a thank-you note to every person they spoke with during their interview. They can also send a written note a few days later.

Many hiring managers say a short, handwritten note that thanks the interviewers for their time makes a favorable impression. It also gives the job seeker a second chance to mention his or her interest in working for the company. And, if the hiring manager is torn between two people, the applicant who follows up with a thank-you note usually tips the odds in his or her favor.

CHAPTER Seven

Watts the Outlook for Electricians?

The outlook for future electricians is pretty bright. The Bureau of Labor Statistics anticipates nearly 115,000 new job openings for qualified electricians by 2022. That is an increase of roughly 20 percent, which is faster than the average growth rate predicted for all occupations.

What is the driving force behind this growth? For one thing, energy experts predict a 35 percent increase in the demand for electricity by 2030, which means an increased demand for electricians as well. On top of this, many older electricians are expected to retire between 2015 and 2020. These two factors could mean a huge shortfall of electricians in many communities.

Evidence of a dwindling supply of electricians is already being seen through the current shortage of available workers in the construction area, which is a large employer of electricians. According to the Associated General Contractors of America (AGC), in August and September of 2014, over one thousand construction firms took part in a nationwide survey. The results

Qualified electricians are in short supply, especially in the construction industry. The growing number of women electricians could help solve this problem.

of that survey showed that more than two-thirds of construction firms across the nation were having difficulty finding electricians and other qualified workers to fill their open positions.

Young people who enter their electrician apprenticeship during this juncture should have no problems finding a job. In fact, they will help fill a need by seeking electrical positions in their communities. Those who are testing this career field by becoming electrician's helpers will also be in high demand. *U.S. News and World Report* lists electrician's helpers in its top one hundred fastest growing jobs. It predicts an increase of about 1,500 helper positions between 2015 and 2022.

Opportunities Abound

The electrical field has many specialties and subspecialties to choose from, particularly with the continuing development of new technologies. For example, in both small towns and large cities, hospitals and doctors' offices are adopting electronic record-keeping systems. Wireless technology has increased the demand everywhere for computers, printers, and other document imaging systems to be integrated. Security systems and voice activated systems are being used in more communities than in the past. Electricians are needed to install, repair, and maintain these systems to help businesses meet the needs of their patients and customers.

A growing number of businesses have employees who avoid long commutes by working from home at least part of the week. The growing use of computers and telecommunication equipment in homes and businesses has increased demand for buildings to be pre-wired during construction. Existing homes and buildings may need to be wired or retrofitted to accommodate the new systems. The increasing use of these systems is creating a need for more VDV and IBS installer technicians to install, repair, and maintain them.

FROM ACTRESS TO ELECTRONICS INVENTOR

Today, many restaurants, hotels, and other businesses advertise the availability of free Wi-Fi to lure customers. And most of us don't go anywhere without our cell phones. But few people know that the technology for cell phones and other wireless devices was developed by a movie actress trying to help her adopted country win a war.

Born in Austria, actress Hedy Lamarr fled to the United States during World War II and became a naturalized citizen. In the 1930s and 1940s, many people thought Lamarr was the most beautiful woman on Hollywood's silver screen. But she is perhaps better known today for her role in developing the electronic technology that made wireless developments like Wi-Fi and cell phones possible.

During World War II, American and other Allied forces were often unsuccessful in torpedoing German submarines because the enemy was able to jam the radio signals that guided the torpedoes. Lamarr developed a system that allowed radio signals to hop quickly from one frequency to another, which prevented radio jamming.

Lamarr teamed up with American composer George Antheil to create a device that could send and receive eighty-eight radio signals that were constantly changing in split-second intervals in a synchronized system. The device was patented in 1942. But it was not used until twenty years later, during the Cuban missile crisis of 1962. Rather than preventing signal jamming, Lamarr's invention was used to provide secure communication between the ships that were involved in the naval blockade. In 1997 Lamarr was honored for her invention by the Electronic Frontier Foundation.

Called "spread spectrum" today, Lamarr's frequency-hopping technology is what makes secure communication possible for cell phones, Wi-Fi, and other wireless communications.

Robotics

In the growing field of robotics, electricians have additional opportunities. Industrial electricians have worked with robotic systems for some time in factories and manufacturing plants. Increasingly, hospitals around the country are using sophisticated robots to assist in delicate surgeries. Robotic and automation systems are also used in hospitals, labs, and pharmacies to measure, weigh, mix, and dispense medications. To fill the growing need for electricians in this area, robotics-related programs are offered at many community colleges and universities. Two of these are Bates Technical College in Tacoma, Washington, which offers a program titled Industrial Electronics and Robotics Technician, and Utah Valley University, which has a program in Electrical Automation and Robotic Technology.

Electricians Are Needed Everywhere

With power demands outstripping the current capacity of many larger cities, there is a continuing need

SUBSTATION DIVISION

Electrical Engineer

Some factories and manufacturing plants operate twenty-four hours a day, seven days a week. They may have several electricians for each shift.

for more generating stations. Because these stations are usually built some distance away from populated areas, high-voltage transmission systems will also need to be built and maintained in order to move electricity from the generating stations to homes and businesses. Outside linemen will be needed to install and maintain these stations as well as the power lines connecting them to communities.

The television and movie industries also depend on electricians. From working on the lighting systems on sets and sound stations to powering massive camera equipment and running electric wind machines, electricians keep the entertainment industry running. In 1997 two electricians—Bill

Communities across the country need qualified electricians to install electric meters in homes and businesses. Meters must also be tested periodically to ensure accuracy.

Masten and Rick Prey—won an Academy Award for technical achievement for developing a mobile lighting system still in use by filmmakers today.

Some electricians specialize in work needed by steel and iron mills; others support the energy needs of the mining industry. Electricians are also needed by theme parks, radio stations, grocery stores, and school districts. And local electric companies in every town and city rely on electricians who specialize in installing, testing, and repairing the power meters that record how much electricity is being used in homes and businesses.

Electricians at military bases across the country fill a wide variety of needs. Some keep the lighting and other equipment in hospitals, barracks, and mess halls functioning. Others install and repair the wiring in repair shops, offices, base stores, and other buildings. Electricians are additionally needed to install, repair, and maintain radio equipment and other communication systems on ships, submarines, and various aircraft.

Never Boring

An electrician may be many things, but one thing he or she never need to be is bored. From the type of industry or business they want to work in to the area they want to specialize in, electricians have many choices. Even their day-to-day tasks are interesting and widely varied. For most electricians, every day brings a new project, a new challenge to be solved, or a new location. And as new technologies are developed and new equipment is invented, there are new things to be learned. The National Electric Code is regularly updated to help keep electricians aware of changes in codes relating to things like the installation of electrical equipment, fiber-optic cables, and signaling and communications conductors.

Electricians can also grow in their careers by advancing to supervisory and management positions, becoming contractors, or by starting their own small business. Some electricians help train future electricians by teaching at CTE and vo-tech schools or local community colleges.

Whether they want to travel around the world with the military, prefer living in a small town, or crave the excitement of a large city, electricians can be sure that they will be needed in every community.

GLOSSARY

APPRENTICESHIP A system of on-the-job training that prepares someone for a particular trade.

BLUEPRINT A technical drawing or diagram of an architectural or engineering plan.

COMMERCIAL Of or relating to a business seeking to make a profit.

CONDUIT A tube or channel that holds electrical wire or cable.

CONTRACTOR A person or company that signs an agreement to perform work.

CPR Cardiopulmonary resuscitation; an emergency treatment for someone whose heart stops beating.

CTE Career and technical education; A program that combines academic classes with technical training needed to enter a particular career field.

DEXTERITY Being able to use one's hands, arms, and legs with skill and coordination.

FIBER OPTICS Transparent glass or plastic fibers that transmit data in the form of light.

GAUGE The thickness of a wire. Gauge also determines the amperage or amount of current the wire can carry.

GED General educational development; a diploma awarded to those who complete a course of academic study similar to that required to earn a high school diploma.

GENERATOR A machine that produces electricity by converting mechanical energy.

GROUNDING CONDUCTOR An electrical wire that safely re-routes current to the ground if there is a circuit fault or over-voltage.

INDUSTRIAL Having to do with the manufacturing of goods or products.

NATIONAL ELECTRIC CODE The standard for the safe
  installation of electrical equipment and electrical
  wiring.

SOLDER To melt a metal or metallic alloy in order to
  join or fuse metallic surfaces.

STAMINA The ability to be physically or mentally active
  for a long period of time.

TRANSFORMER A device that can increase or decrease
  the voltage of an alternating electric current.

UNION A group of workers in a particular industry who
  join together to work for better pay and better
  working conditions.

VOCATIONAL Refers to a course of study that provides
  necessary skills for a particular job or career.

FOR MORE INFORMATION

Canadian Association of Women in Construction
(CAWC)
365 Brunel Road, Unit #1
Mississauga, ON L4Z 1Z5
Canada
(416) 759-1991
Website: http://www.cawic.ca
The CAWC is a nonprofit organization for women
employed in construction and related fields in
Canada. It offers mentorships, job and résumé
postings, and other support.

Canadian Electrical Contractors Association
(CECA)
460-170 Attwell Drive
Toronto, ON M9W 5Z5
Canada
(416) 675-3226
Website: http://www.ceca.org
CECA is comprised of electrical contractor groups
from around Canada that represent the interests
of their members nationally.

Electric Power Research Institute (EPRI)
3420 Hillview Avenue
Palo Alto, CA 94304
Website: http://www.epri.com
The EPRI conducts and disseminates research
about electricity delivery and use to benefit the
public and the electricity industry.

Electrical Training Alliance
301 Prince George's Boulevard, Suite D
Upper Marlboro, MD 20774

(888) 652-4007
Website: http://www.electricaltrainingalliance.org
This alliance has over three hundred joint apprenticeship training centers in the United States
   and Canada. The organization also offers educational resources, including publications and
   support material for teachers and students.

Independent Electrical Contractors (IEC)
4401 Ford Avenue, Suite 1100
Alexandria, VA 22302
(800) 456-4324
Website: http://www.ieci.org
The IEC is the national trade association for merit
   shop electrical and systems contractors. The
   organization has fifty-four chapters across the
   nation.

International Brotherhood of Electrical Workers (IBEW)
900 Seventh Street NW
Washington, DC 20001
(202) 833-7000
Website: http://www.ibew.org
This union represents about 750,000 Canadian
   and U.S. electrical workers. Making it one of the
   largest unions. Its members work in a wide variety of skilled fields.

The International Society of Certified Electronics
   Technicians
3000-A Landers Street
Fort Worth, TX 76107-5642
(800) 946-0201

Website: http://www.iscet.org
This organization offers training and testing to certify a variety of technicians.

Job Corps
200 Constitution Avenue NW, Suite N4463
Washington, DC 20210
(800) 733-5627
Website: http://www.jobcorps.gov
The Job Corps is a free program for young adults aged sixteen to twenty-four that provides education and career training in a variety of fields. Housing and medical and dental care are provided to students during their enrollment with Job Corps.

National Association of Women in Construction
327 S. Adams Street
Fort Worth, TX 76104-1002
(800) 552-3506
Website: http://www.nawic.org
This organization supports women in construction and related fields, including electricians. It provides members with opportunities for professional development and education.

National Electrical Contractors Association (NECA)
3 Bethesda Metro Center, Suite 1100
Bethesda, MD 20814
(301) 657-3110
Website: http://www.necanet.org
The NECA is a national organization that represents and supports electrical contractors.

Tradeswomen, Inc.
1433 Webster Street
Oakland, CA 94612
(510) 891-8773
Website: http://www.tradeswomen.org
This California-based organization supports women
 who work as electricians and in other blue-collar
 careers. It offers information on trainings, apprentice-
 ships, and jobs.

Websites

Because of the changing nature of Internet links,
Rosen Publishing has developed an online list of
websites related to the subject of this book. This
site is updated regularly. Please use this link to
access the list:

http://www.rosenlinks.com/CIYC/Elect

FOR FURTHER READING

Bolles, Richard N. *What Color Is Your Parachute?* New York, NY: Ten Speed Press, 2013.

Carlson, W. Bernard. *Tesla: Inventor of the Electrical Age.* Princeton, NJ: Princeton University Press, 2013.

Committee on the National Electric Code. *NEC 2014: National Electrical Code 2014/NFPA 70 (National Fire Protection Associations National Electrical Code).* Quincy, MA, 2014.

Covey, Sean. *The 7 Habits of Highly Effective Teens.* New York, NY: Touchstone, 2014.

Croft, Terrell, Frederic Harwell, and Wilford Summers. *American Electricians Handbook.* 16th ed. New York, NY: McGraw Hill Professional Publishing, 2013.

Farr, Michael. *100 Fastest-Growing Careers.* Indianapolis, IN: JIST Publishing, 2010.

Geier, Michael J. *How to Diagnose and Fix Everything Electronic.* New York, NY: McGraw Hill, 2011.

Gibilisco, Stan. *Electricity Demystified.* New York, NY: McGraw Hill, 2012.

Harmon, Daniel E. *A Career as an Electrician.* New York, NY: Rosen Publishing, 2011.

Harmon, Daniel E. *Internship & Volunteer Opportunities for Science and Math Wizards.* New York, NY: Rosen Publishing, 2013.

Herman, Stephen. *Delmar's Standard Textbook of Electricity.* 6th ed. Boston, MA: Cengage Learning, 2016.

Herres, David. *The Electrician's Trade Demystified.* New York, NY: McGraw-Hill Professional Publishing, 2013.

Jonnes, Jill. *Empires of Light: Edison, Tesla, Westinghouse, and the Race to Electrify the World.* New York, NY: Random House Publishing Group, 2004.

Kennedy, Joyce Lain. *Resumes for Dummies.* Hoboken, NJ: John Wiley and Sons, Inc., 2011.

Moccio, Fran. *Live Wire: Women and Brotherhood in the Electrical Industry.* Philadelphia, PA: Temple University Press, 2010.

Santiago, John M., Jr. *Circuit Analysis for Dummies.* Hoboken, NJ: John Wiley and Sons, Inc., 2013.

Schepp, Brad, and Debra Schepp. *How to Find a Job on LinkedIn, Facebook, Twitter, MySpace, and Other Social Networks.* New York, NY: McGraw Hill, 2010.

Shatkin, Laurence. *150 Best Jobs for the Military-to-CivilianTransition.* St. Paul, MN: JIST Publishing, 2013.

Shatkin, Laurence. *300 Best Jobs Without a Four-Year Degree.* Indianapolis, IN: JIST Publishing, 2013.

Westscott, Sean, and Jean Riescher Westcott. *The Complete Idiot's Guide to Electronics 101.* New York, NY: Penguin Group, 2011.

BIBLIOGRAPHY

Aquila, Jennifer. Aviation electrician, AAR in Indianapolis, IN. Interview with the author, September 2014.

Associated Press. "Tens of Thousands Still Powerless in South After Ice Storm." *USA Today*, February 18, 2014. Retrieved September 20, 2014 (http://www.usatoday.com/story/weather/2014/02/18/thousands-still-without-power-south-carolina-georgia-ice-storm/5580887).

Bureau of Labor Statistics. "Electricians." *Occupational Outlook Handbook, 2014-2015 Edition.* 2014. Retrieved September 20, 2014 (http://www.bls.gov/ooh/construction-and-extraction/electricians.htm).

Doucette, Calli. IBEW apprentice, Canada. Interview with the author, October 2014.

Ghose, Tia. "Nikola Tesla vs. Thomas Edison: Who Was the Better Inventor?" *Live Science*, July 10, 2014. Retrieved September 20, 2014 (http://www.livescience.com/46739-tesla-vs-edison-comparison.html).

Goelling, R. Tarn. District of Columbia Young Trade Unionists, chair. Interview with the author, October 2014.

Gray, Julie. *Interview Success—Get the Edge.* London, England: Hodder Education, 2011.

Greeley, Joann. Journeyman electrician, Newfoundland, Canada. Interview with the author, October 2014.

Grensing-Pophal, Lin. *The Everything Job Interview Book.* Avon, MA: Adams Media, 2012.

Huebner, Dustin. "Get the Right Tools for the Job." Retrieved September 18, 2014 (http://www.electricianinformationresource.com/discover-tools/electrical-tool-kit).

Kleiner, Morris M., and Kyoung Won Park. "Life, Limbs, and Licensing: Occupational Regulation, Wages,

and Workplace Safety of Electricians, 1992-2007."
Monthly Labor Review, January 2014. Retrieved
September 20, 2014 (http://www.bls.gov/mlr/2014/
article/life-limbs-and-licensing-1.htm).

Lee, Christopher. Owner, Electrical Etc. in Arizona.
Interview with the author, October 2014.

Leibman, Pete. *I Got My Dream Job and So Can
You.* New York, NY: American Management
Association, 2012.

Los Angeles Times Staff. "Napa Earthquake: Power
Restored to Thousands; Cleanup Continues." *Los
Angeles Times*, August 25, 2014. Retrieved
September 20, 2014 (http://www.latimes.com/
local/lanow/la-me-ln-napa-earthquake-power
-restored-20140825-story.html).

McGeehan, Patrick. "Demand for Electricians Soars
After Hurricane Sandy." *New York Times*,
November 20, 2012. Retrieved September 27, 2014
(http://www.nytimes.com/2012/11/21/nyregion/
demand-for-electricians-soars-after-hurricane
-sandy.html?_r=0).

National Institute for Occupational Safety and Health.
"Young Worker Safety and Health." June 23, 2014.
Retrieved October 10, 2014 (http://www.cdc.gov/
niosh/topics/youth).

O-Net OnLine. "Summary Report for Electricians."
Retrieved September 27, 2014 (http://www
.onetonline.org/link/summary/47-2111.00).

Rivas, Mia. Journeyman inside wireman, California.
Interview with the author, October 2014.

Westcott, Sean, and Jean Riescher Westscott. *The
Complete Idiot's Guide to Electronics 101*. New
York, NY: Penguin Group, 2011.

INDEX

ABOUT THE AUTHOR

Bobi Martin's interest in electricians began with her stepfather, who was an electrician in the navy. Serving as a Lt. Radioman during World War II, he survived an ambush in France where he earned a Purple Heart. Martin is the author of several nonfiction books, a former magazine columnist, and a library media specialist. She earned a MFA in writing from Vermont College of Fine Arts and was named Member of the Year for 1994 by the Society of Children's Book Writers and Illustrators. She loves to travel and has taught writing workshops across the United States and in Okinawa, Japan.

Photo Credits

Designer: Nicole Russo; Editor: Shalini Saxena